THE SANITY OF ART

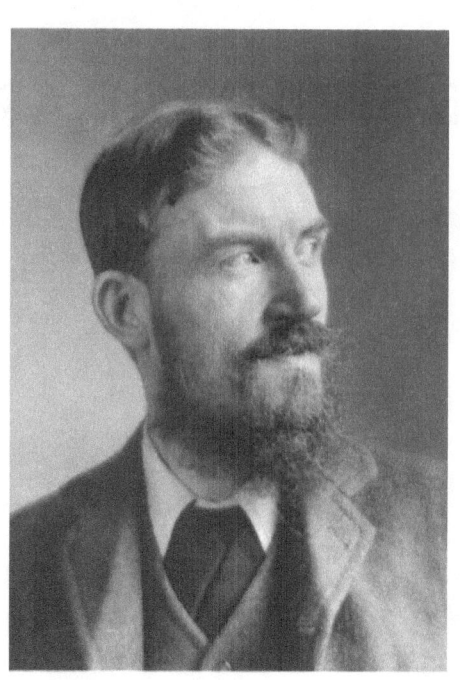

THE SANITY OF ART

George Bernard Shaw

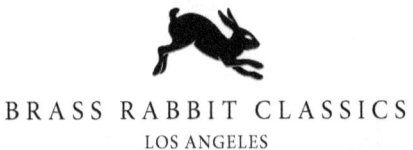

BRASS RABBIT CLASSICS

LOS ANGELES

TITLE:
THE SANITY OF ART
(1895)

AUTHOR:
GEORGE BERNARD SHAW
(1856-1950)

EDITOR:
MARK DIEDERICHSEN

PUBLISHER:
BRASS RABBIT CLASSICS
Los Angeles, California

FIRST BRASS RABBIT CLASSICS EDITION

FIRST PRINTING:
2014

FRONT COVER:
JAMES ABBOTT MCNEILL WHISTLER
(1834-1903)
Jo
1861
etching and drypoint
cancelled plate
Los Angeles County Museum of Art

BACK COVER:
BERTHA NEWCOMBE
(1857-1947)
George Bernard Shaw
1892
oil on canvas

FRONTISPIECE:
FREDERICK HENRY EVANS
(1852-1943)
George Bernard Shaw
1894
photograph

ISBN-TEN: 0692280391
ISBN-THIRTEEN: 978-0692280393

Contents

PREFACE

The re-publication of this open letter to Mr. Benjamin Tucker, places me, not for the first time, in the difficulty of the journalist whose work survives the day on which it was written. What the journalist writes about is what everybody is thinking about (or ought to be thinking about) at the moment of writing. To revive his utterances when everybody is thinking about something else; when the tide of public thought and imagination has turned; when the front of the stage is filled with new actors; when many lusty crowers have either survived their vogue or perished with it; when the little men you patronized have become great, and the great men you attacked have been sanctified and pardoned by popular sentiment in the tomb: all these inevitables test the quality of your journalism very severely.

Nevertheless, journalism is the highest form of literature; for all the highest literature is journalism. The writer who aims at producing the platitudes which are "not for an age, but for all time" has his reward in being unreadable in all ages; whilst Plato and Aristophanes trying to knock some sense into the Athens of their day, Shakespeare peopling that same Athens with Elizabethan mechanics and Warwickshire hunts, Ibsen photographing the local doctors and vestrymen of a Norwegian parish, Carpaccio painting the life of St. Ursula exactly as if she were a lady living in the next street to him, are still alive and at home everywhere among the dust and ashes of thousands of academic, punctilious, archaeologically correct men of letters and art who spent their lives haughtily avoiding the journalist's vulgar obsession with the ephemeral.

I also am a journalist, proud of it, deliberately cutting out of my works all that is not journalism, convinced that nothing that is not journalism will live long as literature, or be of any use whilst it does live. I deal with all periods; but I never study any period but the present, which I have not yet mastered and never shall; and as a dramatist I have no clue to any historical or other personage save that part of him which is also myself, and which may be nine tenths of him or ninety-nine hundredths, as the case may be (if, indeed, I do not transcend the creature), but which, anyhow, is all that can ever come within my knowledge of his soul. The man who writes about himself and his own time is the only man who writes about all people and about all time. The. other sort of man, who believes that he and his period are so distinct from all other men and periods that it would be immodest and irrelevant to allude to them or assume that they could interest anyone but himself and his contemporaries, is the most infatuated of all the egotists, and consequently the most unreadable and negligible of all the authors. And so, let others cultivate what they call literature: journalism for me!

The following remnant of the journalism of 1895 will, I hope, bear out these preliminary remarks, which are none the less valid because they are dragged in here to dismount the critics who ride the high horse of Letters at me. It was undertaken under the following circumstances. In 1893 Doctor Max Nordau, one of those remarkable cosmopolitan Jews who go forth against modern civilization as David went against the Philistines or Charles Martel against the Saracens, smiting it hip and thigh without any sense of common humanity with it, trumped up an indictment of its men of genius as depraved lunatics, and pled it (in German) before the bar of Europe under the title Entartung. It was soon translated for England and America as Degeneration. Like all rigorous and thorough-going sallies of special pleading, it has its value; for the way to get at the merits of a case is not to listen to the fool who imagines himself impartial, but to get it argued with reckless bias for and against. To understand a saint, you must hear the devil's advocate; and the same is true of the artist. Nordau had briefed himself as devil's advocate against the great artistic reputations of the XIX century; and he did his duty as well as it could be done at the price, incidentally saying many more true and important things than most of the counsel on the other side were capable of.

Indeed counsel on the other side mostly threw up their briefs in consternation, and began to protest that they entirely agreed with Dr. Nordau, and that though they had perhaps dallied a little with Rossetti, Wagner, Ibsen, Tolstoy, Nietzsche and the rest of the degenerates before their true character had been exposed, yet they had never really approved of them. Even those who stood to their guns had not sufficient variety of culture to contradict the cosmopolitan doctor on more than one or two points, being often not champions of Art at large, but merely jealous fanciers of some particular artist. Thus the Wagnerians were ready to give up Ibsen; the Ibsenites were equally suspicious of Wagner; the Tolstoyans gave up both; the Nietzscheans were only too glad to see Tolstoy catching it; and the connoisseurs of Impressionism in painting, though fairly impartial in music and literature, could not handle the technics of the case for them. Yet Dr. Nordau's case was so bad, and his technical utterances on painting and music so much more absurd than Captain Lemuel Gulliver's nautical observations, that I, being familiar with all the arts, and accustomed to the revolutionary climate of Jewish cosmopolitanism, looked on at his triumph much as Napoleon looked on at the massacre of the Swiss, thinking how easy it would be to change the rout into the cheapest of victories. However, none of our silly editors had the gumption to offer me the command; so, like Napoleon, I went home and left them to be cut to pieces.

But Destiny will not allow her offers to be completely overlooked. In the Easter of 1895, when Nordau was master of the field, and the newspaper champions of modem Literature and Art were on their knees before him, weeping and protesting their innocence, I was staying in the wooden hotel on Beachy Head, with a select party of Fabians, politicians, and philosophers, diligently trying to ride a bicycle for the first time in my life. My efforts set the coast-guards laughing as no audience had ever laughed at my plays. I made myself ridiculous with such success that I felt quite ready to begin on somebody else. Just then there arrived a proposal from Mr. Benjamin Tucker, philosophic Anarchist, and editor of an American paper called Liberty, which, as it was written valiantly up to its title, was having a desperate struggle for existence in a country where every citizen is free to suppress liberty, and usually does so in such moments as he cares to spare from the pursuit of money. Mr. Tucker, seeing that nobody had answered Dr. Nordau, and perceiving with the penetration of an unterrified common-sense that a doctor who had written manifest nonsense must be answerable technically by anybody who could handle his weapons, was of opinion that I was the man to do it. Accordingly, said Mr. Tucker, I invite you, Shaw, to ascertain the highest price that has ever been paid to any man, even to Gladstone, for a magazine article; and I will pay you that price for a review of Degeneration in the columns of Liberty.

This was really great editing. Mr. Tucker got his review, as he deserved, and sent a copy of the number of Liberty containing it (now a collector's treasure), to every paper in the United States. There was a brisk and quick sale of copies in London among the cognoscenti. And Degeneration was never heard of again. It is open to the envious to contend that this was a mere coincidence— that the Degeneration boom was exhausted at that moment; but I naturally prefer to believe that Mr. Tucker and I slew it. I may add that the slaughter incidentally ruined Mr. Tucker, as a circulation among cognoscenti does not repay the cost of a free distribution to the Philistines; but Mr. Tucker was always ruining himself for Liberty and always retrieving the situation by his business ability. I saw him this year in London, as prosperous looking a man as I could desire to dine with, and eager for fresh struggles with the courts and public departments of the United States.

It may now be asked why, if the work of my essay be done, I need revive it after twelve years of peaceful burial. I should answer: partly because Mr. Tucker wishes to reproduce his editorial success in a more permanent form, and is strongly seconded by Messrs.

Holbrook Jackson and A. R. Orage in England, who have piously preserved a copy of Liberty and desire to make it the beginning of their series of pamphlets in connection with their paper The New Age and their pet organization, The Arts Group of the Fabian Society; partly because on looking through it myself again, I find that as far as it goes it is still readable and likely to be helpful to those who are confused by the eternal strife between the artist-philosophers and the Philistines.

I have left the essay substantially as it first appeared, the main alteration being an expansion of the section dealing with the importance of the mass of law which lies completely outside morals and religion, and is really pure convention: the point being, not that the course prescribed by such law is ethically right, or indeed better in any sense than its direct opposite (as in the rule of the road, for example), but that it is absolutely necessary for economy and smoothness of social action that everybody should do the same thing and be able to count on everybody else doing it. I have appropriated this from Mr. Aylmer Maude's criticism of Tolstoy an Anarchism, on which I am unable to improve.

I have also, with the squeamishness of advancing years, softened one or two expressions which now shock me as uncivil to Dr. Nordau. In doing so I am not offering him the insult of an attempt to spare his feelings: I am simply trying to mend my own manners.

Finally, let me say that though I think this essay of mine did dispose of Dr. Nordau's special pleadings, neither the pleadings nor the criticism dispose of the main question as to how far genius is a morbid symptom. I should rather like Dr. Nordau to try again; for I do not see how any observant student of genius from the life can deny that the Arts have their criminals and lunatics as well as their sane and honest men (they are more or less the same men too, just as our ordinary criminals are in the dock by the accident of a single transaction and not by a difference in nature between them and the judge and jury), and that the notion that the great poet and artist can do no wrong is as mischievously erroneous as the notion that the King can do no wrong or that the Pope is infallible or that the power which created all three did not do its own best for them.

In my last play, The Doctor's Dilemma, I have emphasized this by dramatizing a rascally genius, with the disquieting result that several intelligent and sensitive persons have passionately defended him, on the ground, apparently, that high artistic faculty and an ardent artistic imagination entitle a man to be recklessly dishonest about money and recklessly selfish about women just as kingship in an African tribe entitles a man to kill whom he pleases on the most trifling provocation. I know no harder practical question than how much selfishness one ought to stand from a gifted person for the sake of his gifts or on the chance of his being right in the long run. The Superman will certainly come like a thief in the night, and be shot at accordingly; but we cannot leave our property wholly undefended on that account. On the other hand, we cannot ask the Superman simply to add a higher set of virtues to current respectable morals; for he is undoubtedly going to empty a good deal of respectable morality out like so much dirty water, and replace it by new and strange customs, shedding old obligations and accepting new and heavier ones. Every step of his progress must horrify conventional people; and if it were possible for even the most superior man to march ahead all the time, every pioneer of the march towards the Superman would be crucified. Fortunately what actually happens is that your geniuses are for the most part keeping step and marking time with the rest, an occasional stumble forward being the utmost they can accomplish, often visibly against their own notions of propriety. The greatest possible difference in conduct between a genius and his contemporaries is so small that it is always difficult to persuade the people who are in daily contact with the gifted one that he is anybody in particular: all the instances to the contrary (Gorki scandalizing New York, for example) being cases in which the genius is in conflict, not with contemporary feeling in his own class, but with some institution which is far behind the times, like the institution of marriage in Russia (to put it no nearer home). In really contemporary situations, your genius is ever 1 part genius and 99 parts Tory. Still, especially when we turn from conduct to the expression of opinion—from what the man of genius dares do to what he dares advocate—it is necessary for the welfare of society that genius should be privileged to utter sedition, to blaspheme, to outrage good taste, to corrupt the youthful mind, and, generally, to scandalize its uncles. But as such license is accordable only on the assumption that men of genius are saner, sounder, farther sighted and deeper fathoming than the uncles, it is idle to demand unlimited toleration of apparently outrageous conduct on the plea that the offender is a genius, even when by the abnormal development of some specific talent he may be highly skilled as an artist. Andrea del Sarto was a better draughtsman and fresco painter than Raphael; but he was a swindler all the same; and no honorable artist would plead on his behalf that misappropriating trust money is one of the superiorities of that very loosely defined diathesis which we call the artistic temperament. If Dr. Nordau would make a serious attempt to shew us exactly where we are in this matter by ascertaining the real stigmata of genius, so that we may know whom to crucify, and whom to put above the law, he will place the civilization he attacks under an obligation which will wipe out the marks of all the wounds (mostly thoroughly deserved) he has dealt it.

London, July, 1907.

THE SANITY OF ART

INTRODUCTION

My dear Tucker:

I have read Max Nordau's Degeneration at your request: two hundred and sixty thousand mortal words, saying the same thing over and over again. That is the proper way to drive a thing into the mind of the world, though Nordau considers it a symptom of insane "obsession" on the part of writers who do not share his own opinions. His message to the world is that all our characteristically modern works of art are symptoms of disease in the artists, and that these diseased artists are themselves symptoms of the nervous exhaustion of the race by overwork.

To me, who am a professional critic of art, and have for many successive London seasons had to watch the grand march past of books, of pictures, of concerts and operas, and of stage plays, there is nothing new in Dr. Nordau's outburst. I have heard it all before. At every new wave of energy in art the same alarm has been raised; and as these alarms always had their public, like prophecies of the end of the world, there is nothing surprising in the fact that a book which might have been produced by playing the resurrection man in the old newspaper rooms of our public libraries, and collecting all the exploded bogey-criticisms of the last half-century into a huge volume, should have a considerable success. To give you an idea of the heap of material ready to hand for such a compilation, let me lay before you a sketch of one or two of the Reformations I have myself witnessed in the fine arts.

IMPRESSIONISM

When I was engaged chiefly in the criticism of pictures, the Impressionist movement was struggling for life in London; and I supported it vigorously because, being the outcome of heightened attention and quickened consciousness on the part of its disciples, it was evidently destined to improve pictures greatly by substituting a natural, observant, real style for a conventional, taken-for-granted, ideal one. The result has entirely justified my choice of sides. I can remember when Mr. Whistler, in order to force the public to observe the qualities he was introducing into pictorial work, had to exhibit a fine drawing of a girl with the head deliberately crossed out with a few rough pencil strokes, knowing perfectly well that if he left a woman's face discernible the British Philistine would simply look to see whether she was a pretty girl or not, or whether she represented some of his pet characters in fiction, and pass on without having seen any of the qualities of artistic execution which made the drawing valuable. But it was easier for the critics to resent the obliteration of the face as an insolent eccentricity, and to shew their own good manners by writing of Mr. Whistler as Jimmy, than to think out what he meant. It took several years of "propaganda by deed" before the qualities which the Impressionists insisted on came to be looked for as matter of course in pictures; so that at last the keen picture-gallery frequenter, when he came face to face with

Bouguereau's Girl in a Cornfield, could no longer accept it as a window-glimpse of nature, but saw at a glance that the girl is really standing in a studio with what the house agents call a good north light, and that the cornfield is a conventional sham. This advance in the education of our art fanciers was effected by persistently exhibiting pictures which, like Mr. Whistler's girl with her head scratched out, were propagandist samples of workmanship rather than complete works of art. But the moment Mr. Whistler and his party forced the dealers and the societies of painters to exhibit these studies, and, by doing so, to accustom the public to tolerate what appeared to it at first to be absurdities, the door was necessarily opened to real absurdities. It is exceedingly difficult to draw or paint well: it is exceedingly easy to smudge paper or canvas so as to suggest a picture just as the stains on an old ceiling or the dark spots in a glowing coal-fire do. Plenty of rubbish of this kind was produced, exhibited, and tolerated at the time when people could not see the difference between any daub in which there were aniline shadows and a landscape by Monet. Not that they thought the daub as good as the Monet: they thought the Monet as ridiculous as the daub; but they were afraid to say so, because they had discovered that people who were good judges did not think Monet ridiculous.

Then, besides the mere impostors, there were certain unaffected and conscientious painters who produced abnormal pictures because they saw abnormally. My own sight happens to be " normal" in the oculist's sense: that is, I see things with ihe naked eye as most people can only be made to see them by the aid of spectacles. Once I had a discussion with an artist who was shewing me a clever picture of his in which the parted lips in a pretty woman's face revealed what seemed to me like a mouthful of virgin snow. The painter lectured me for not consulting my eyes instead of my knowledge of facts. "You don't see the divisions in a set of teeth when you look at a person's mouth," he said: "all you see is a strip of white, or yellow, or pearl, as the case may be. But because you know, as a matter of anatomic fact, that there are divisions there, you want to have them represented by strokes in a drawing. That is just like you art critics etc., etc." I do not think he believed me when I told him that when I looked at a row of teeth, I saw, not only the divisions between them, but their exact shape, both in contour and in modelling, just as well as I saw their general color. Some of the most able of the Impressionists evidently did not see forms as definitely as they appreciated color relationship; and, since there is always a great deal of imitation in the arts, we soon had young painters with perfectly good sight looking at landscapes or at their models with their eyes half closed and a little asquint, until what they saw looked to them like one of their favorite master's pictures.

Further, the Impressionist movement led to a busy study of the atmosphere, conventionally supposed to be invisible, but seldom really completely so, and of what were called values; that is, the relation of light and dark between the various objects depicted, on the correctness of which relation truth of effect largely depends. This, though very difficult in full out-door light with the various colors brilliantly visible, was comparatively easy in gloomy rooms where the absence of light reduced all colors to masses of brown or grey of varying depth. Whistler's portrait of Sarasate, a masterpiece in its way, would look like a study in monochrome if hung beside a portrait of Holbein; and the little bouquets of color with which he sometimes decorates his female sitters, exquisite as the best of them are, have the character of enamel, of mosaic, of jewelry: never of primitive nature. His disciples could paint dark interiors, or figures placed apparently in coal cellars, with admirable truth and delicacy of values whilst they were still helplessly unable to represent a green tree or a blue sky, much less paint an interior with the light and local color as clear as they are in the works of Peter de Hooghe. Naturally the public eye, with its utilitarian familiarity with local color, and its Philistine insensibility to values and atmosphere, did not at first see what the Impressionists were driving at, and dismissed them as mere perverse, notoriety-hunting cranks.

Here, then, you had a movement wholly beneficial and progressive, and in no sense insane or decadent. Nevertheless it led to the public exhibition of daubs which even the authors themselves would never have presumed to offer for exhibition before; it betrayed aberrations of vision in painters who, on the old academic lines, would have hidden their defects by drawing objects (teeth for instance) as they knew them to exist, and not as they saw them; it set clear-sighted students practising optical distortion, so as to see things myopically and astigmatically; and it substituted canvasses which looked like enlargements of under-exposed photographs for the familiar portraits of masters of the hounds in cheerfully unmistakable pink coats, mounted on bright chestnut horses. All of which, and much else, to a man who looked on without any sense of the deficiencies in conventional painting, necessarily suggested that the Impressionists and their contemporaries were much less sane than their fathers.

WAGNERISM

Again, my duties as a musical critic compelled me to ascertain very carefully the exact bearings of the controversy which has raged round Wagner's music-dramas since the middle of the century. When you and I last met, we were basking in the sun between the acts of Parsifal at Bayreuth; but experience has. taught me that an American may appear at Bayreuth without being necessarily fonder than most men of a technical discussion on music. Let me therefore put the case to you in a mercifully intelligible way. Music is like drawing, in that it can be purely decorative, or purely dramatic, or anything between the two. A draughtsman may be a pattern-designer like William Morris, or he may be a delineator of life and character, like Ford Madox Brown. Or he may come between these two extremes, and treat scenes of life and character in a decorative way, like Walter Crane or Burne-Jones: both of them consummate pattern-designers, whose subject-pictures and illustrations are also fundamentally figure-patterns, prettier than Madox Brown's, but much less convincingly alive. Do you realize that in music we have these same alternative applications of the art to drama and decoration? You can compose a graceful, symmetrical sound-pattern that exists solely for the sake of its own grace and symmetry. Or you can compose music to heighten the expression of human emotion; and such music will be intensely affecting in the presence of that emotion, and utter nonsense apart from it. For examples of pure pattern-designing in music I should have to go back to the old music of the thirteenth, fourteenth, and fifteenth centuries, before the operatic movement gained the upper hand; but I am afraid my assertions that much of this music is very beautiful and hugely superior to the stuff our music publishers turn out to-day would not be believed in America; for when I hinted at something of the kind lately in the American Musical Courier, and pointed out also the beauty of the instruments for which this old music was written (viols, virginals, and so on), one of your leading musical critics rebuked me with an expatiation on the superiority (meaning apparently the greater loudness) of the modern concert grand pianoforte, and contemptuously ordered the Middle Ages out from the majestic presence of the nineteenth century.* You must take my word for it that in England alone a long line of composers, from Henry VIII to Lawes and Purcell, have left us quantities of instrumental music which was neither dramatic music nor descriptive music, but was designed to affect the hearer solely by its beauty of sound and grace and ingenuity of pattern. This is the art which Wagner called absolute music. It is represented to-day by the formal sonata and symphony; and we are coming back to it in something like its old integrity by a post-Wagnerian reaction led by that greatly gifted absolute musician and hopelessly commonplace and tedious homilist, Johannes Brahms.

To understand the present muddle, you must know that modern

---

* Perhaps by this time, however, Mr. Arnold Dolmetsch has educated America in this matter, as he educated London and educated me.

dramatic music did not appear as an independent branch of musical art, but as an adulteration of decorative music. The first modern dramatic composers accepted as binding on them the rules of good pattern-designing in sound; and this absurdity was made to appear practicable by the fact that Mozart had such an extraordinary command of his art that his operas contain numbers which, though they seem to follow the dramatic play of emotion and character without reference to any other consideration whatever, are seen, on examining them from the point of view of the absolute musician, to be perfectly symmetrical sound-patterns. But these *tours de force* were no real justification for imposing the laws of pattern-designing on other dramatic musicians; and even Mozart himself broke away from them in all directions, and was violently attacked by his contemporaries for doing so, the accusations levelled at him (absence of melody, illegitimate and discordant harmonic progressions, and monstrous abuse of the orchestra) being sxactly those with which the opponents of Wagner so often pester ourselves. Wagner, whose leading lay characteristic was his enormous common-sense, completed the emancipation of the dramatic musician from these laws of pattern-designing; and we now have operas, and very good ones too. written by composers like Bruneau, who are not musicians in the old sense at all: that is, they are not pattern-designers; they do not compose music apart from drama; and when they have to furnish their operas with dances, instrumental intermezzos or the like, they either take themes from the dramatic part of their operas and rhapsodize on them, or else they turn out some perfectly simple song or dance tune, at the cheapness of which Haydn would have laughed, and give it an air of momentousness by orchestral and harmonic fineries. If I add now that music in the academic, professorial, Conservative, respectable sense always means decorative music, and that students are taught that the laws of pattern-designing are binding on all musicians, and that violations of them are absolutely "wrong "; and if I mention incidentally that these laws are themselves confused by the survivals from a still older tradition based on the Church art, technically very highly specialized, of writing perfectly smooth and beautiful vocal harmony for unaccompanied voices, worthy to be sung by angelic doctors round the throne of God (this was Palestrina's art), you will understand why all the professional musicians who could not see beyond the routine they were taught, and all the men and women (and there are many of them) who have little or no sense of drama, but a very keen sense of beauty of sound and prettiness of pattern in music, regarded Wagner as a madman who was reducing music to chaos, perversely introducing ugly and brutal sounds into a region where beauty and grace had reigned alone, and substituting an incoherent, aimless, formless, endless meandering for the old familiar symmetrical tunes like Pop Goes the Weasel, in which the second and third lines repeat, or nearly repeat, the pattern of the first and second; so that any one can remember and treasure them like nursery rhymes. It was the unprofessional, "unmusical" public which caught the dramatic clue, and saw order and power, strength and sanity, in the supposed Wagner chaos; and now, his battle being won and overwon, the professors, to avert the ridicule of their pupils, are compelled to explain (quite truly) that Wagner's technical procedure in music is almost pedantically logical and grammatical; that the Lohengrin and Tristan preludes are masterpieces of the form proper to their aim; and that his disregard of "false relations," and his free use of the most extreme discords without "preparation," are straight and sensible instances of that natural development of harmony which has proceeded continuously from the days when common six-four chords were considered "wrong," and such free use of unprepared dominant sevenths and minor ninths as had become common in Mozart's time would have seemed the maddest cacophony.*

The dramatic development also touched purely instrumental music. Liszt tried hard to extricate himself from pianoforte arabesques, and become a tone poet like his friend Wagner. He wanted his symphonic poems to express emotions and their development. And he defined the emotion by connecting it with some

---

* As I spent the first twenty years of my life in Ireland I am, for the purposes of this survey of musical art, at least a century and a half old. I can remember the sensation given by the opening chord of Beethoven's youthful Prometheus overture. It sounded strangely strong and momentous, because the use of the third inversion of the chord of the dominant seventh without preparation was unexpected in those days. As to exploding undiminished chords of the ninth and thirteenth on the unsuspecting ear in the same way (everybody does it nowadays), one might as well have sat down on the keyboard and called it music. The very name of the thirteenth was inconceivable: a discreetly prepared and resolved suspension of "four to threes" was the only form in which that discord was known. I can remember, too, the indignation with which Macfarren, after correcting his pupils for unintentional consecutive fifths all his life, found himself expected to write an analytic program for the performance at a Philharmonic concert of an overture by a composer (Goetz) who actually wrote consecutive sevenths intentionally because he liked them.

However, I do not insert this note for the sake of my reminiscences, but because, since writing the text above, a composer of the first order (Richard Strauss) has become known in London, and has been attacked, just as Wagner was, by the very men who lived through the huge blunder of anti-Wagnerism. This cannot be accounted for by the superstitions of the age of decorative music. Every critic nowadays is thoroughly inured to descriptive and dramatic music which is not only as independent of the old decorative forms as Strauss's, but a good deal more so; for Strauss lives on the verge of a barcarolle and seldom resists a nursery tune for long. The hostility to him may be partly due to the fact that by his great achievement of rescuing music from the realm of tights and wigs and stage armor in which Wagner, with all his genius, dwelt to the last, and bringing it into direct contact with modern life, he was enabled in his Heldenleben to give an orchestral caricature of his critics which comes much closer home than Wagner's medievally disguised Beckmesser. But Strauss is denounced by men who are quite capable of laughing at themselves, who are sincere advocates of modern realism in other arts, and who are sufficiently good judges to know, for instance, that the greater popularity of Tchaikowsky is

known story, poem, or even picture: Mazeppa, Victor Hugo's Les Preludes, Kaulbach's Die Hunnenschlacht, or the like. But the moment you try to make an instrumental composition follow a story, you are forced to abandon the decorative pattern forms, since all patterns consist of some form which is repeated over and over again, and which generally consists in itself of a repetition of two similar halves. For example, if you take a playing-card (say the five of diamonds) as a simple example of a pattern, you find not only that the diamond figure is repeated five times, but that each side of each pip is a reversed duplicate of the other. Now, the established form for a symphony is essentially a pattern form involving just such symmetrical repetitions; and, since a story does not repeat itself, but pursues a continuous chain of fresh incident and correspondingly varied emotions Liszt, had either to find a new

---

like the popularity of Rossini nearly a century ago; that is, the vogue of a musical Byron, who, though very pleasant in his lighter vein, very strenuous in his energetic vein, and at least grandiose in his sublime vein, never attains, or desires to attain, the elevation at which the great modern musicians from Bach to Strauss maintain themselves. Anti-Straussism is therefore accounted for neither by the old anti-Wagnerian confusion nor by the petulance of the critic who is beaten by his job.

I conclude that the disagreeable effect which an unaccustomed discord produces on people who cannot divine its resolution is to blame for most of the nonsense now written about Strauss. Strauss's technical procedure involves a profusion of such shocks. But the disagreeable effect will not last. There is no longer a single discord used by Wagner of which the resolution is not already as much a platitude as the resolution of the simple sevenths of Mozart and Meyerbeer. Strauss not only goes from discord to discord, leaving the implied resolutions to be inferred by people who never heard them before, but actually makes a feature of unresolved discords, just as Wagner made a feature of unprepared ones. Men who were reconciled quite late in life to compositions beginning with dominant thirteenths *fortissimo,* find themselves disquieted now by compositions ending with unresolved tonic sevenths.

I think this phase of protest will soon pass. I think so because I find myself able to follow Strauss's harmonic procedure; to divine the destination of his most discordant passing phrases (it is too late now to talk of mere "passing notes"); and to tolerate his most offhand ellipses and most unceremonious omissions of final concords with enjoyment, though my musical endowment is none of the acutest. In twenty years the complaints about his music will be as unintelligible as the similar complaints about Handel, Mozart, Beethoven, and Wagner in the past.

I must apologize for the technical jargon I have had to use in this note. Probably it is all obsolete by this time; but I know nothing newer. Stainer would have understood it thirty years ago. If nobody understands it to-day, my knowledge will seem all the more profound.

musical form for his musical poems, or else face the intolerable anomalies and absurdities which spoil the many attempts made by Mendelssohn, Raff and others, to handcuff the old form to the new matter. Consequently he invented the symphonic poem, a perfectly simple and fitting common-sense form for his purpose, and one which makes Les Preludes much plainer sailing for the ordinary hearer than Mendelssohn's Melusine overture or Raffs Lenore or Im Walde symphonies, in both of which the formal repetitions would stamp Raff as a madman if we did not know that they were mere superstitions, which he had not the strength of mind to shake off as Lizst did. But still, to the people who would not read Liszt's explanations and cared nothing for his purpose, who had no taste for symphonic poetry, and consequently insisted on judging the symphonic poems as sound-patterns, Liszt must needs appear, like Wagner, a perverse egotist with something fundamentally disordered in his intellect: in short, a lunatic.

The sequel was the same as in the Impressionist movement. Wagner, Berlioz, and Liszt, in securing tolerance for their own works, secured it for what sounded to many people absurd; and this tolerance necessarily extended to a great deal of stuff which was really absurd, but which the secretly-bewildered critics dared not denounce, lest it, too, should turn out to be great, like the music of Wagner, over which they had made the most ludicrous exhibition of their incompetence. Even at such stupidly conservative concerts as those of the London Philharmonic Society I have seen ultra-modern composers, supposed to be representatives of the Wagnerian movement, conducting pretentious rubbish in no essential superior to Jullien's British- Army Quadrilles. And then, of course, there are the young imitators, who are corrupted by the desire to make their harmonies sound like those of the masters whose purposes and principles of work they are too young to understand, and who fall between the old forms and the new into simple incoherence.

Here, again, you see, you have a progressive, intelligent, wholesome, and thoroughly sane movement in art, producing plenty of evidence to prove the case of any clever man who does not understand music, but who has a theory which involves the proposition that all the leaders of the art movements of our time are degenerate and, consequently, retrogressive lunatics.

IBSENISM

There is no need for me to go at any great length into the grounds on which any development in our moral views must at first appear insane and blasphemous to people who are satisfied, or more than satisfied, with the current morality. Perhaps you remember the opening chapters of my Quintessence of Ibsenism, in which I shewed why the London press, now abjectly polite to Ibsen, received him four years ago with a shriek of horror. Every step in morals is made by challenging the validity of the existing conception of perfect propriety of conduct; and when a man does that, he must look out for a very different reception from the painter who has ventured to paint a shadow brilliant lilac, or the composer who ends his symphony with an unresolved discord. Heterodoxy in art is at worst rated as eccentricity or folly: heterodoxy in morals is at once rated as scoundrelism, and, what is worse, propagandist scoundrelism, which must, if successful, undermine society and bring us back to barbarism after a period of decadence like that which brought imperial Rome to its downfall. Your function as a philosophic Anarchist in American society is to combat the attempts that are constantly being made to arrest development by using the force of the State to suppress all departures from what the majority consider to be "right" in conduct or overt opinion. I dare say you find the modern democratic voter a very troublesome person, chicken-heartedly diffident as to the value of his opinions on the technics of art or science, about which he may learn all that there is to be known, but cocksure about right and wrong in morals, politics, and religion, about which he can at best only guess at the depth and danger of his ignorance. Happily, this cocksureness is not confined to the Conservatives. Shelley is as cocksure as the dons who expelled him from Oxford. It is true that the revolutionist of twenty-five, who sees nothing for it but a clean sweep of all our institutions, finds himself, at forty, accepting and even clinging to them on condition of a few reforms to bring them up to date. But he does not wait patiently for this reconciliation. He expresses his (or her) early dissatisfaction with the wisdom of his elders loudly and irreverently, and formulates his heresy as a faith. He demands the abolition of marriage, of the State, of the Church; he preaches the divinity of love and the heroism of the man who believes in himself and dares do the thing he wills; he contemns the slavery to duty and discipline which has left so many soured old people with nothing but envious regrets for a virtuous youth. He recognizes his gospel in such utterances as that quoted by Nordau from Brandes: "To obey one's senses is to have character. He who allows himself to be guided by his passions has individuality." For my part, I am not at all afraid of this doctrine, either in Brandes's form or in the older form: "He that is unjust, let him be unjust still; and he which is filthy, let him be filthy still; and he that is righteous, let him be righteous still; and he that is holy, let him be holy still." But Nordau expresses his horror of Brandes with all the epithets he can command; "debauchery, dissoluteness, depravity disguised as modernity, bestial instincts, *maitre de plaisir,* egomaniacal Anarchist," and such sentences as the following:

> It is comprehensible that an educator who turns the school-room into a tavern and a brothel should have success and a crowd of followers. He certainly runs the risk of being slain by the parents if they come to know what he is teaching their children; but the pupils will hardly complain, and will be eager to attend the lessons of so agreeable a teacher. This is the explanation of the influence Brandes gained over the youth of his country, such as his writings, with their emptiness of thought and unending tattle, would certainly never have procured for him.

To appreciate this spluttering, you must know that it is immediately followed by an attack on Ibsen for the weakness of " obsession by the doctrine of original sin." Yet what would the passage I have just quoted be without the doctrine of original sin as a postulate? If " the heart of man is deceitful above all things, and desperately wicked," then, truly, the man who allows himself to be guided by his passions must needs be a scoundrel; and his teacher might well be slain by his parents. But how if the youth thrown helpless on his passions found that honesty, that self-respect, that hatred of cruelty and injustice, that the desire for soundness and health and efficiency, were master passions: nay, that their excess is so dangerous to youth that it is part of the wisdom of age to say to the young: "Be not righteous overmuch: why shouldst thou destroy thyself?" I am sure, my dear Tucker, your friends have paraphrased that in vernacular American often enough in remonstrating with you for your Anarchism, which defies not only God, but even the wisdom of the United States Congress. On the other hand, the people who profess to renounce and abjure their own passions, and ostentatiously regulate their conduct by the most convenient interpretation of what the Bible means, or, worse still, by their ability to find reasons for it (as if there were not excellent reasons to be found for every conceivable course of conduct, from dynamiting and vivisection to martyrdom), seldom need a warning against being righteous overmuch, their attention, indeed, often needing a rather pressing jog in the opposite direction.

Passion is the steam in the engine of all religious and moral systems. In so far as it is malevolent, the religions are malevolent too, and insist on human sacrifices, on hell, wrath, and vengeance. You cannot read Browning's Caliban upon Setebos, or, Natural Theology on the Island without admitting that all our religions have been made as Caliban made his, and that the difference between Caliban and Prospero is not that Prospero has killed passion in himself whilst Caliban has yielded to it, but that Prospero is mastered by holier passions than Caliban's. Abstract principles of conduct break down in practice because kindness and truth and justice are not duties founded on abstract principles external to man, but human passions, which have, in their time, conflicted with higher passions as well as with lower ones. If a young woman, in a mood of strong reaction against the preaching of duty and self-sacrifice and the rest of it, were to tell me that she was determined not to murder her own instincts and throw away her life in obedience to a mouthful of empty phrases, I should say to her: "By all means do as you propose. Try how wicked you can be: it is precisely the same experiment as trying how good you can be. At worst you will only find out the sort of person you really are. At best you will find that your passions, if you really and honestly let them all loose impartially, will discipline you with a severity which your conventional friends, abandoning themselves to the mechanical routine of fashion, could not stand for a day." As a matter of fact, we have seen over and over again this comedy of the "emancipated "young enthusiast flinging duty and religion, convention and parental authority, to the winds, only to find herself, for the first time in her life, plunged into duties, responsibilities, and sacrifices from which she is often glad to retreat, after a few years wearing down of her enthusiasm, into the comparatively loose life of an ordinary respectable woman of fashion.

WHY LAW IS INDISPENSABLE

The truth is, laws, religions, creeds, and systems of ethics, instead of making society better than its best unit, make it worse than its average unit, because they are never up to date. You will ask me: "Why have them at all?" I will tell you. They are made necessary, though we all secretly detest them, by the fact that the number of people who can think out a line of conduct for themselves even on one point is very small, and the number who can afford the time for it still smaller. Nobody can afford the time to do it on all points. The professional thinker may on occasion make his own morality and philosophy as the cobbler may make his own boots; but the ordinary man of business must buy at the shop, so to speak, and put up with what he finds on sale there, whether it exactly suits him or not, because he can neither make a morality for himself or do without one. This typewriter with which I am writing is the best I can get; but it is by no means a perfect instrument; and I have not the smallest doubt that in fifty years time authors will wonder how men could have put up with so clumsy a contrivance. When a better one is invented I shall buy it: until then, not being myself an inventor, I must make the best of it, just as my Protestant and Roman Catholic and Agnostic friends make the best of their imperfect creeds and systems. Oh, Father Tucker, worshipper of Liberty, where shall we find a land where the thinking and moralizing can be done without division of labor?

Besides, what have deep thinking and moralizing to do with the most necessary and least questionable side of law? Just consider how much we need law in matters which have absolutely no moral bearing at all. Is there anything more aggravating than to be told, when you are socially promoted, and are not quite sure how to behave yourself in the circles you enter for the first time, that good manners are merely a matter of good sense, and that rank is but the guinea's stamp: the man's the gowd for a' that? Imagine taking the field with an army which knew nothing except that the soldier's duty is to defend his country bravely, and think, not of his own safety, nor of home and beauty, but of ENGLAND! Or of leaving the traffic of Piccadilly or Broadway to proceed on the understanding that every driver should keep to that side of the road which seemed to him to promote the greatest happiness of the greatest number. Or of stage-managing Hamlet by assuring the Ghost that whether he entered from the right or the left could make no difference to the greatness of Shakespeare's play, and that all he need concern himself about was holding the mirror up to nature! Law is never so necessary as when it has no ethical significance whatever, and is pure law for the sake of law. The law that compels me to keep to the left when driving along Oxford Street is ethically senseless, as is shewn by the fact that keeping to the right answers equally well in Paris; and it certainly destroys my freedom to choose my side; but by enabling me to count on everyone else keeping to the left also, thus making traffic possible and safe, it enlarges my life and sets my mind free for nobler issues. Most laws, in short, are not the expression of the ethical verdicts of the community, but pure etiquette and nothing else. What they express is the fact that over most of the field of social life there are wide limits within which it does not matter what people do, though it matters enormously whether under given circumstances you can depend on their all doing the same thing. The wasp, who can be depended on absolutely to sting you if you squeeze him, is less of a nuisance than the man who tries to do business with you not according to the customs of business, but according to the Sermon on the Mount, or than the lady who dines with you and refuses, on republican and dietetic principles, to allow precedence to a duchess or to partake of food which contains uric acid. The ordinary man cannot get through the world without being told what to do at every turn, and basing such calculations as he is capable of on the assumption that everyone else will calculate on the same assumptions. Even your man of genius accepts a hundred rules for every one he challenges; and you may lodge in the same house with an Anarchist for ten years without noticing anything exceptional about him. Martin Luther, the priest, horrified the greater half of Christendom by marrying a nun, yet was a submissive conformist in countless ways, living orderly as a husband and father, wearing what his bootmaker and tailor made for him, and dwelling in what the builder built for him, although he would have died rather than take his Church from the Pope. And when he got a" Church made by himself to his liking, generations of men calling themselves Lutherans took that Church from him just as unquestioningly as he took the fashion of his clothes from his tailor. As the race evolves, many a convention which recommends itself by its obvious utility to everyone passes into an automatic habit, like breathing. Doubtless also an improvement in our nerves and judgment may enlarge the list of emergencies which individuals may be trusted to deal with on the spur of the moment without reference to regulations; but a ready-made code of conduct for general use will always be needed as a matter of overwhelming convenience by all members of communities.

The continual danger to liberty created by law arises, not from the encroachments of Governments, which are always regarded with suspicion, but from the immense utility and consequent popularity of law, and the terrifying danger and obvious inconvenience of anarchy; so that even pirates appoint and obey a captain. Law soon acquires such a good character that people will believe no evil of it; and at this point it becomes possible for priests and rulers to commit the most pernicious crimes in the name of law and order. Creeds and laws come to be regarded as applications to human conduct of eternal and immutable principles of good and evil; and breakers of the law are abhorred as sacrilegious scoundrels to whom nothing is sacred. Now this, I need not tell you, is a very serious error. No law is so independent of circumstances that the time never comes for breaking it, changing it, scrapping it as obsolete, and even making its observance a crime. In a developing civilization nothing can make laws tolerable unless their changes and modifications are kept as closely as possible on the heels of the changes and modifications in social conditions which development involves. Also there is a bad side to the very convenience of law. It deadens the conscience of individuals by relieving them of the moral responsibility of their own actions. When this relief is made as complete as possible, it reduces a man to a condition in which his very virtues are contemptible. Military discipline, for example, aims at destroying the individuality and initiative of the soldier whilst increasing his mechanical efficiency, until he is simply a weapon with the power of hearing and obeying orders. In him you have legality, duty, obedience, self-denial, submission to external authority, carried as far as it can be carried; and the result is that in England, where military service is voluntary, the common soldier is less respected than any other serviceable worker in the community. The police constable is a free civilian who has to use his own judgment and act on his own responsibility in innumerable petty emergencies, and is by comparison a popular and esteemed citizen. The Roman Catholic peasant who consults his parish priest instead of his conscience, and submits wholly to the authority of his Church, is mastered and governed either by statesmen and cardinals who despise his superstition, or by Protestants who are at least allowed to persuade themselves that they have arrived at their religious opinions through the exercise of their private judgment. The moral evolution of the social individual is from submission and obedience as economizers of effort and responsibility, and safeguards against panic and incontinence, to wilfulness and self-assertion made safe by reason and self-control, just as plainly as his physical growth leads from the perambulator and the nurse's apron-string to the power of walking alone, and from the tutelage of the boy to the responsibility of the man. But it is useless for impatient spirits (you and I, for instance) to call on people to walk before they can stand. Without high gifts of reason and self-control: that is, without strong common-sense, no man dare yet trust himself out of the school of authority. What he does is to claim gradual relaxations of the discipline, so as to have as much liberty as he thinks is good for him, and as much government as he thinks he needs to keep him straight. If he goes too fast, he soon finds himself asking helplessly "What ought I to do?"; and so, after running to the doctor, the lawyer, the expert, the old friend, and all the other quacks for advice, he runs back to the law again to save him from all these and from himself. The law may be wrong; but at least it spares him the responsibility of choosing, and will either punish those who make him look ridiculous by exposing its folly, or, when the constitution is too democratic for this, at least guarantee that the majority is on his side.

We see this in the history of British-American Christianity. Man, as the hero of that history, starts by accepting as binding on him the revelation of God's will as interpreted by the Church. Finding his confidence, or rather his intellectual laziness, grossly abused by the Church, he claims a right to exercise his own judgment, which the Reformed Church, competing with the Unreformed for clients, grants him on condition that he arrive at the same conclusions as itself. Later on he violates this condition in certain particulars, and dissents, flying to America in the Mayflower from the prison of Conformity, but promptly building a new jail, suited to the needs of his sect, in his adopted country. In all these mutinies he finds excellent arguments to prove that he is exchanging a false authority for *the* true one, never daring even to think of brazenly admitting that what he is really doing is substituting his own will, bit by bit, for what he calls the will of God or the laws of Nature. These arguments so accustom the world to submit authority to the test of discussion that he is at last emboldened to claim the right to do anything he can find good arguments for, even to the extent of questioning the scientific accuracy of the Book of Genesis, and the validity of the popular conception of God as an omniscient, omnipotent, and frightfully jealous and vindictive old gentleman sitting on a throne above the clouds. This seems a giant stride towards emancipation; but it leaves our hero, as Rationalist and Materialist, regarding Reason as a creative dynamic motor, independent of and superior to his erring passions, at which point it is easy for the Churches to suggest that if Reason is to decide the matter perhaps the conclusions of an Ecumenical Council of learned and skilled churchmen might be more trustworthy than the first crop of cheap syllogisms excogitated by a handful of raw Rationalists in their sects of "Freethinkers" and "Secularists" and "Positivists" or "Don't Knowists" (Agnostics).

Yet it was not the churches, but that very freethinking philosopher Schopenhauer who re-established the old theological doctrine that reason is no motive power; that the true motive power in the world is will (otherwise Life); and that the setting-up of reason above will is a damnable error. But the theologians could not open their arms to Schopenhauer, because he fell into the Rationalist-commercial error of valuing life according to its profits in individual pleasure, and of course came to the idiotic pessimist conclusion that life is not worth living, and that the will which urges us to live in spite of this is necessarily a malign torturer, or at least a bad hand at business, the desirable end of all things being the Nirvana of the stilling of the will and the consequent setting of life's sun "into the blind cave of eternal night." Further, the will of the theologians was the will of a God standing outside man and in authority above him, whereas the Schopenhauerian will is a purely secular force of nature, attaining various degrees of organization, here as a jelly-fish, there as a cabbage, more complexly as an ape or a tiger, and attaining its highest (and most mischievous) form so far in the human being. As to the Rationalists, they approved of Schopenhauer's secularism and pessimism, but of course could not stomach his metaphysical method or his dethronement of reason by will. Accordingly, his turn for popularity did not come until after Darwin's, and then mostly through the influence of two great artists, Richard Wagner and Ibsen, whose Tristan and Emperor and Galilean shew that Schopenhauer was a true pioneer in the forward march of the human spirit. We can now, as soon as we are strong-minded enough, drop the Nirvana nonsense, the pessimism, the rationalism, the supernatural theology, and all the other subterfuges to which we cling because we are afraid to look life straight in the face and see in it, not the fulfilment of a moral law or of the deductions of reason, but the satisfaction of a passion in us of which we can give no account whatever.

It is natural for man to shrink from the terrible responsibility thrown on him by this inexorable fact. All his stock excuses vanish before it: "The woman tempted me," "The serpent tempted me," "I was not myself at the time," "I meant well," "My passion got the better of my reason," "It was my duty to do it," "The Bible says that we should do it," "Everybody does it," and so on. Nothing is left but the frank avowal: "I did it because I am built that way." Every man hates to say that. He wants to believe that his generous actions are characteristic of him, and that his meannesses are aberrations or concessions to the force of circumstances. Our murderers, with the assistance of the jail chaplain, square accounts with the devil and with God, never with themselves. The convict gives every reason for his having stolen something except the reason that he is a thief. Cruel people flog their children for their children's good, or offer the information that a guinea-pig perspires under atrocious torture as an affectionate contribution to science. Lynched negroes are riddled by dozens of superfluous bullets, every one of which is offered as the expression of a sense of outraged justice and chastity in the scamp and libertine who fires it. And such is the desire of men to keep one another in countenance that they positively demand such excuses from one another as a matter of public decency. An uncle of mine, who made it a rule to offer tramps a job when they begged from him, naturally very soon became familiar with every excuse that human ingenuity can invent for not working. But he lost his temper only once; and that was with a tramp who frankly replied that he was too lazy. This my uncle described with disgust as "cynicism." And yet our family arms bear the motto, in Latin, "Know thyself."

As you know, the true trend of this movement has been mistaken by many of its supporters as well as by its opponents. The ingrained habit of thinking of the propensities of which we are ashamed as " our passions," and our shame of them and our propensities to noble conduct as a negative and inhibitory department called generally our conscience, leads us to conclude that to accept the guidance of our passions is to plunge recklessly into the insupportable tedium of what is called a life of pleasure. Reactionists against the almost equally insupportable slavery of what is called a life of duty are nevertheless willing to venture on these terms.' The revolted daughter, exasperated at being systematically lied to by her parents on every subject of vital importance to an eager and intensely curious young student of life, allies herself with really vicious people and with humorists who like to shock the pious with gay paradoxes, in claiming an impossible license in personal conduct. No great harm is done beyond the inevitable and temporary excesses produced by all reactions; for, as I have said, the would-be wicked ones find, when they come to the point, that the indispensable qualification for a wicked life is not freedom but wickedness. But the misunderstanding supports the clamor of the opponents of the newest opinions, who naturally shriek as Nordau shrieks in the passages about. Brandes, quoted above. Thus you have here again a movement which is thoroughly beneficial and progressive presenting a hideous appearance of moral corruption and decay, not only to our old-fashioned religious folk, but to our comparatively modern scientific Rationalists as well. And here again, because the press and the gossips have found out that this apparent corruption and decay is considered the right thing in some influential quarters, and must be spoken of with respect, and patronized and published and sold and read, we have a certain number of pitiful imitators taking advantage of their tolerance to bring out really silly and rotten stuff, which the reviewers are afraid to expose, lest it, too, should turn out to be the correct thing.

After this long preamble, you will have no difficulty in understanding the sort of book Nordau has written. Imagine a huge volume, stuffed with the most slashing of the criticisms which were hurled at the Impressionists, the Tone Poets, and the philosophers and dramatists of the Schopenhauerian revival, before these movements had reached the point at which it began to require some real courage to attack them. Imagine a rehash not only of the newspaper criticisms of this period, but of all its little parasitic paragraphs of small-talk and scandal, from the long-forgotten jibes against Oscar Wilde's momentary attempt to bring knee-breeches into fashion years ago, to the latest scurrilities about "the New Woman." Imagine the general staleness and occasional putrescence of this mess disguised by a dressing of the terminology invented by Krafft-Ebing, Lombroso, and all the latest specialists in madness and crime, to describe the artistic faculties and propensities as they operate in the insane. Imagine all this done by a man who is a vigorous and capable journalist, shrewd enough to see that there is a good opening for a big reactionary book as a relief to the Wagner and Ibsen booms, bold enough to let himself go without respect to persons or reputations, lucky enough to be a stronger, clearer-headed man than ninety-nine out of a hundred of his critics, besides having a keener interest in science: a born theorist, reasoner, and busybody; therefore able, without insight, or even any very remarkable intensive industry (he is, like most Germans, extensively industrious to an appalling degree), to produce a book which, has made a very considerable impression on the artistic ignorance of Europe and America. For he says a thing as if he meant it; he holds superficial ideas obstinately, and sees them clearly; and his mind works so impetuously that it is a pleasure to watch it— for a while. All the same, he is the dupe of a theory which would hardly impose on one of those gamblers who have a system or martingale founded on a solid rock of algebra, by which they can infallibly break the bank at Monte Carlo. "Psychiatry" takes the place of algebra in Nordau's martingale.

This theory of his is, at bottom, nothing but the familiar delusion of the used-up man that the world is going to the dogs. But Nordau is too clever to be driven back on ready-made mistakes: he makes them for himself in his own way. He appeals to the prodigious extension of the quantity of business a single man can transact through* the modern machinery of social intercourse: the railway, the telegraph and telephone, the post, and so forth. He gives appalling statistics of the increase of railway mileage and shipping, of the number of letters written per head of the population, of the newspapers which tell us things (mostly lies) of which we used to know nothing.* "In the last fifty years," he says, "the population of Europe has not doubled, whereas the sum of its labors has increased tenfold: in part, even fifty-fold. Every civilized man furnishes, at

---

* Perhaps I had better remark in passing that, unless it were true — which it is not — that the length of the modern penny letter or halfpenny post-card is the same as that of the eighteenth-century letter, and that the number of persons who know how to read and write has not increased, there is no reason whatever to draw Nordau's conclusion from the postal statistics.

the present time, from five to twenty-five times as much work as was demanded of him half a century ago."** Then follow more statistics of " the constant increase of crime, madness, and suicide," of increases in the mortality from diseases of the nerves and heart, of increased consumption of stimulants, of new nervous diseases like "railway spine and railway brain," with the general moral that we are all suffering from exhaustion, and that symptoms of degeneracy are visible in all directions, culminating at various points in such hysterical horrors as Wagner's music, Ibsen's dramas, Manet's pictures, Tolstoy's novels, Whitman's poetry, Dr. Jaeger's woollen clothing, vegetarianism, scepticism as to vivisection and vaccination, Anarchism and humanitarianism, and, in short, everything that Dr. Nordau does not happen to approve of.

You will at once see that such a case, if well got up and argued, is worth hearing, even though its advocate has no chance of a verdict, because it is sure to bring out a certain number of interesting and important facts. It is, I take it, quite true that with our railways and our postal services many of us are for the moment very like a pedestrian converted to bicycling, who, instead of using his machine to go twenty miles with less labor than he used to walk seven, proceeds to do a hundred miles instead, with the result that the "labor-saving" contrivance acts as a means of working its user to exhaustion. It is also true that under our existing industrial system

---

** Here again we have a statement which means nothing unless it be compared with statistics as to the multiplication of the civilized man's power of production by machinery, which in some industries has multiplied a single man's power by hundreds and in others by thousands. As to crimes and disease, Nordau should state whether he counts convictions under modern laws— for offences against the Joint Stock Company Acts, for instance— as proving that we have degenerated since those Acts were passed, and whether he regards the invention of new names for a dozen varieties of fever which were formerly counted as one single disease as an evidence of decaying health in the face of the increasing duration of life.

machinery in industrial processes is regarded solely as a means of extracting a larger product from the unremitted toil of the actual wage-worker. And I do not think any person who is in touch with the artistic professions will deny that they are recruited largely by persons who become actors, or painters, or journalists and authors because they are incapable of steady work and regular habits, or that the attraction which the patrons of the stage, music, and literature find in their favorite arts has often little or nothing to do with the need which nerves great artists to the heavy travail of creation. The claim of art to our respect must stand or fall with the validity of its pretension to cultivate and refine our senses and faculties until seeing, hearing, feeling, smelling, and tasting become highly conscious and critical acts with us, protesting vehemently against ugliness, noise, discordant speech, frowzy clothing, and re-breathed air, and taking keen interest and pleasure in beauty, in music, and in nature, besides making us insist, as necessary for comfort and decency, on clean, wholesome, handsome fabrics to wear, and utensils of fine material and elegant workmanship to handle. Further, art should refine our sense of character and conduct, of justice and sympathy, greatly heightening our self-knowledge, self-control, precision of action, and considerateness, and making us intolerant of baseness, cruelty, injustice, and intellectual superficiality or vulgarity. The worthy artist or craftsman is he who serves the physical and moral senses by feeding them with pictures, musical compositions, pleasant houses and gardens, good clothes and fine implements, poems, fictions, essays, and dramas which call the heightened senses and ennobled faculties into pleasurable activity. The great artist is he who goes a step beyond the demand, and, by supplying works of a higher beauty and a higher interest than have yet been perceived, succeeds, after a brief struggle with its strangeness, in adding this fresh extension of sense to the heritage of the race. This is why we value art: this is why we feel that the iconoclast and the Philistine are attacking something made holier, by solid usefulness, than their own theories of purity and practicality: this is why art has won the privileges of religion; so that London shopkeepers who would fiercely resent a compulsory church rate, who do not know Yankee Doodle from Luther's hymn, and who are more interested in photographs of the latest celebrities than in the Velasquez portraits in the National Gallery, tamely allow the London County Council to spend their money on bands, on municipal art inspectors, and on plaster casts from the antique.

But the business of responding to the demand for the gratification of the senses has many grades. The confectioner who makes unwholesome sweets, the bullfighter, the women whose advertisements in the American papers are so astounding to English people, are examples ready to hand to shew what the art and trade of pleasing may be, not at its lowest, but at the lowest that we can speak of without intolerable shame. We have dramatists who write their lines in such a way as to enable low comedians of a certain class to give them an indecorous turn; we have painters who aim no higher than Giulio Romano did when he decorated the Palazzo Te in Mantua; we have poets who have nothing to versify but the commonplaces of amorous infatuation; and, worse than all the rest put together, we have journalists who openly profess that it is their duty to "reflect" what they believe to be the ignorance and prejudice of their readers, instead of leading and enlightening them to the best of their ability: an excuse for cowardice and time-serving which is also becoming well worn in political circles as "the duty of a democratic statesman." In short, the artist can be a prostitute, a pander, and a flatterer more easily, as far as external pressure goes, than a faithful servant of the community, much less the founder of a school or the father of a church. Even an artist who is doing the best he can may be doing a very low class of work: for instance, many performers at the rougher music-halls, who get their living by singing coarse songs in the rowdiest possible way, do so to the utmost of their ability in that direction in the most conscientious spirit of earning their money honestly and being a credit to their profession. And the exaltation of the greatest artists is not continuous: you cannot defend every line of Shakespeare or every stroke of Titian. Since the artist is a man and his patron a man, all human moods and grades of development are reflected in art; consequently the iconoclast's or the Philistine's indictments of art have as many counts as the misanthrope's indictment of humanity. And this is the Achilles heel of art at which Nordau has struck. He has piled the iconoclast on the Philistine, the Philistine on the misanthrope, in order to make out his case.

ECHOLALIA

L et me describe to you one or two of his artifices as a special pleader making the most of the eddies at the sides of the stream of progress. Take as a first specimen the old and effective trick of pointing out, as "stigmata of degeneration" in the person he is abusing, features which are common to the whole human race. The drawing-room palmist astonishes ladies by telling them "secrets" about themselves which are nothing but the inevitable experiences of ninety-nine people out of every hundred, though each individual is vain enough to suppose that they are peculiar to herself. Nordau turns the trick inside out by trusting to the fact that people are in the habit of assuming that uniformity and symmetry are laws of nature: for example, that every normal person's face is precisely symmetrical, that all persons have the same number of bones in their bodies, and so on. He takes advantage of this popular error to claim asymmetry as a stigma of degeneration. As a matter of fact, perfect symmetry or uniformity does not exist in nature. My two profiles, when photographed, are hardly recognizable as belonging to the same person by those who do not know me; so that the camera would prove me an utter degenerate if my case were exceptional. Probably, however, you would not object to testify that my face is as symmetrical as faces are ordinarily made. Another unfailing trick is the common one of having two names for the same thing, one abusive, the other complimentary, for use according to circumstances. You know how it is done: "We trust the Government will be firm" in one paper, and " We hope the obstinate elements in the Cabinet will take warning in time" in another. The following is a typical specimen of Nordau's use of this device. First, let me explain that when a man with a turn for rhyming goes mad, he repeats rhymes as if he were quoting a rhyming dictionary. You say "Come" to him, and he starts away with " Dumb, plum, sum, rum, numb, gum," and so on. This the doctors call echolalia. Dickens gives a specimen of it in Great Expectations, where Mr. Jaggers's Jewish client expresses his rapture of admiration for the lawyer by exclaiming: "Oh, Jaggerth, Jaggerth, Jaggerth! all otherth ith Cag-Maggerth: give me Jaggerth!" There are some well-known verses by Swinburne, beginning, "If love were what the rose is," which, rhyming and tripping along very prettily, express a sentiment without making any intelligible statement whatsoever; and we have plenty of nonsensically inconsequent nursery rhymes, like Ba, ba, black sheep, or Old Daddy long legs, which please sane children just as Mr. Swinburne's verses please sane adults, simply as funny or pretty little word-patterns. People do not write such things for the sake of conveying information, but for the sake of amusing and pleasing, just as people do not eat strawberries and cream to nourish their bones and muscles, but to enjoy the taste of a toothsome dish. A lunatic may plead that he eats kitchen soap and tin tacks on the same ground; and, as far as I can see, the lunatic would completely shut up Nordau by this argument; for Nordau is absurd enough, in the case of rhyming, to claim that every rhyme made for its own sake, as proved by the fact that it does not convey an intelligible statement of fact of any kind, convicts the rhymer of echolalia. He can thus convict any poet whom he dislikes of being a degenerate by simply picking out a rhyme which exists for its own sake, or a pun, or what is called a burden in a ballad, and claiming them as symptoms of echolalia, supporting this diagnosis by carefully examining the poem for contradictions and inconsistencies as to time, place, description, or the like. It will occur to you probably that by this means he must bring out Shakespeare as the champion instance of poetic degeneracy, since Shakespeare was an incorrigible punster; delighted in burdens (for instance, "With hey, ho, the wind and the rain," which exactly fulfils all the conditions accepted by Nordau as symptomatic of insanity in Rossetti's case); and rhymed for the sake of rhyming in quite a childish fashion; whilst, as to contradictions and inconsistencies, A Midsummer Night's Dream, as to which Shakespeare never made up his mind whether the action covered a week or a single night, is only one of a dozen instances of his slips. But no: Shakespeare, not being a nineteenth-century poet, would have spoiled the case for modern degeneration by showing that its symptoms existed before the telegraph and the railway were dreamt of; and besides, Nordau likes Shakespeare, just as he likes Goethe, and holds him up as a model of sanity in contrast to the nineteenth-century poets. Thus Wagner is a degenerate because he made puns; and Shakespeare, who made worse ones, is a great poet. Swinburne, with his "unmeaning" refrains of "Small red leaves in the mill water," and "Apples of gold for the King's daughter," is a diseased madman; but Shakespeare, with his " In spring time, the only merry ring time, when birds do sing hey ding a ding ding" (if this is not the worst case of echolalia in the world, what *is* echolalia?), is a sober master mind, Rossetti, with his Blessed Damozel leaning out from the gold bar of heaven, weeping though she is in paradise, which is a happy place; describing the dead in one line as "dressed in white" and in another as "mounting like thin flames"; and calculating days and years quite otherwise than commercial almanacks do, is that dangerous and cranky thing, a mystic; whilst Goethe (the author of the second part of Faust, if you please) is a hard-headed, accurate, sound, scientific poet. As to the list of inconsistencies of, which poor Ibsen is convicted, it is too long to be dealt with in detail. But I assure you I am not doing Nordau less than justice when I say that if he had accused Shakespeare of inconsistency on the ground that Othello is represented in the first act as loving his wife, and in the last as strangling her, the demonstration would have left you with more respect for his good sense than his pages on Ibsen, the folly of which goes beyond all patience.*

When Nordau deals with painting and music, he is less irritating, because he errs through ignorance, and ignorance, too, of a sort that is now perfectly well recognized and understood. We all know what the old-fashioned critic of literature and science who cultivated his detective logic without ever dreaming of cultivating his eyes and

---

* Perhaps I had better give one example. Nordau first quotes a couple of speeches from An Enemy of the People and The Wild Duck:

Stockmann: I love my native town so well that I had rather ruin it than see it nourishing on a lie. All men who live on lies must be exterminated like vermin. (An Enemy of the People.)

Relling: Yes, I said, illusion [lie]. For illusion, you know, is the stimulating principle. Rob the average man of his life illusion and you rob him of his happiness at the same time. (The Wild Duck.)

Nordau proceeds to comment as follows:

"Now, what is Ibsen's real opinion? Is a man to strive for truth or to swelter in deceit? Is Ibsen with Stockmann or with Relling? Ibsen owes us an answer to these questions or, rather, he replies to them affirmatively and negatively with equal ardor and equal poetic power."

ears, can be relied upon to say when painters and composers are under discussion. Nordau gives himself away with laughable punctuality. He celebrates "the most glorious period of the Renaissance" and "the rosy dawn of the new thought" with all the gravity of the older editions of Murray's guides to Italy. He tells us that "to copy Cimabue and Giotto is comparatively easy: to imitate Raphael it is necessary to be able to draw and paint to perfection." He lumps Fra Angelico with Giotto and Cimabue, as if they represented the same stage in the development of technical execution, and Pollajuolo with Ghirlandajo. "Here," he says, speaking of the great Florentine painters, from Giotto to Masaccio, "were paintings bad in drawing, faded or smoked, their coloring either originally feeble or impaired by the action of centuries, pictures *executed with the awkwardness of a learner* . . . easy of imitation, since, in painting pictures in the style of the early masters, faulty drawing, deficient sense of color, and *general artistic incapacity,* are so many advantages." To make any comment on these howlers would be to hit a man when he is down. Poor Nordau offers them as a demonstration that Ruskin, who gave this sort of ignorant nonsense its deathblow in England, was a delirious mystic. Also that Millais and Holman Hunt, in the days of the pre-Raphaelite brotherhood, strove to acquire the qualities of the early Florentine masters because the Florentine easel pictures were so much easier to imitate than those of the apprentices in Raphael's Roman fresco factory.

In music we find Nordau equally content with the theories as to how music is composed which were current among literary men fifty years ago. He tells us of "the severe discipline and fixed rules of the theory of composition, which gave a grammar to the musical babbling of primeval times, and made of it a worthy medium for the expression of the emotions of civilized men," and describes Wagner as breaking these fixed rules and rebelling against this severe discipline because he was "an inattentive mystic, abandoned to amorphous dreams." This notion that there are certain rules, derived from a science of counterpoint, by the application of which pieces of music can be constructed just as an equilateral triangle can be constructed on a given straight line by any one who has mastered Euclid's first proposition, is highly characteristic of the generation of blind and deaf critics to which Nordau belongs. It is evident that if there were fixed rules by which Wagner or anyone else could have composed good music, there could have been no more severe discipline in the work of composition than in the work of arranging a list of names in alphabetical order. The severity of artistic discipline is produced by the fact that in creative art no ready-made rules can help you. There is nothing to guide you to the right expression for your thought except your own sense of beauty and fitness; and, as you advance upon those who went before you, that sense of beauty and fitness is necessarily often in conflict, not with fixed rules, because there are no rules, but with precedents, which are what Nordau means by fixed rules, as far as he knows what he is talking about enough to mean anything at all. If Wagner had composed the prelude to Das Rheingold with a half close at the end of the eighth bar and a full close at the end of the sixteenth, he would undoubtedly have followed the precedent of Mozart and other great composers, and complied with the requirements of Messrs. Hanslick, Nordau and Company. Only, as it happened, that was not what he wanted to do. His purpose was to produce a tone picture of the mighty flood in the depths of the Rhine; and, as the poetic imagination does not conceive the Rhine as stopping at every eight feet to take off its hat to Herren Hanslick and Nordau, the closes and half closes are omitted, and Nordau, huffed at being passed by as if he were a person of no consequence, complains that the composer is "an inattentive mystic, abandoned to amorphous dreams." But, even if Wagner's descriptive purpose is left out of the question, Nordau's general criticism of him is an ignorant one; for the truth is that Wagner, like most artists who have great intellectual power, was dominated in the technical work of his gigantic scores by so strong a regard for system, order, logic, symmetry, and syntax, that when in the course of time his melody and harmony become perfectly familiar to us, he will be ranked with Handel as a composer whose extreme regularity of procedure must make his work appear drily mechanical to those who cannot catch its dramatic inspiration. If Nordau, having no sense of that inspiration, had said: "This fellow, whom you all imagine to be the creator of a new heaven and a new earth in music out of a chaos of poetic emotion, is really an arrant pedant and formalist," I should have pricked up my ears and listened to him with some curiosity, knowing how good a case a really keen technical critic could make out for that view. As it is, I have only to expose him as having picked up a vulgar error under the influence of a vulgar literary superstition. For the rest, you will hardly need any prompting of mine to appreciate the absurdity of dismissing as "inattentive" the Paris journalist, the Dresden conductor, the designer and founder of the Bayreuth enterprise, the humorous and practical author of On Conducting, and the man who scored and stagemanaged the four evenings of The Niblung's Ring. I purposely leave out the composer, the poet, the philosopher, the reformer, since Nordau cannot be compelled to admit that Wagner's eminence in these departments was real. Striking them all out accordingly, there remain the indisputable, objective facts of Wagner's practically professional ability and organizing power to put Nordau's diagnosis of Wagner as an amorphous, inattentive person out of the question. If Nordau had one hundredth part of the truly terrific power of attention which Wagner must have maintained all his life almost as easily as a common man breathes, he would not now be so deplorable an example of the truth of his own contention that the power of attention may be taken as the measure of mental strength.

Nordau's trick of calling rhyme echolalia when he happens not to like the rhymer is reapplied in the case of authorship, which he calls graphomania when he happens not to like the author. He insists that Wagner, who was a voluminous author as well as a composer, was a graphomaniac; and his proof is that in his books we find "the restless repetition of one and the same strain of thought . . . Opera and Drama, Judaism in Music, Religion and the State, Art and Religion, and the Vocation of Opera are nothing more than the amplification of single passages in The Art-Work of the Future." This is a capital example of Nordau's limited power of attention. The moment that limited power is concentrated on his theory of degeneration, he loses sight of everything else, and drives his one borrowed horse into every obstacle on the road. To those of us who can attend to more than one thing at a time, there is no observation more familiar, and more frequently confirmed, than that this growth of pregnant single sentences into whole books which Nordau discovers in Wagner, balanced as it always is by the contraction of whole boyish chapters into single epigrams, is the process by which all great writers, speakers, artists, and thinkers elaborate their life-work. Let me take a writer after Nordau's own heart, a specialist in lunacy, one whom he quotes as a trustworthy example of what he calls "the clear, mentally sane author, who, feeling himself impelled to say something, once for all expresses himself as distinctly and impressively as it is possible for him to do, and has done with it": namely, Dr. Henry Maudsley. Dr. Maudsley is a clever and cultivated specialist in insanity, who has written several interesting books, consisting of repetitions, amplifications, and historical illustrations of the same idea, which is. if I may put it rather more bluntly than the urbane author, nothing less than the identification of religious with sexual ecstasy. And the upshot of it is the conventional scientific pessimism, from which Dr. Maudsley never gets away; so that his last book repeats his first book, instead of leaving it far behind, as Wagner's State and Religion leaves his Art and Revolution behind. But now that I have prepared the way by quoting Dr. Maudsley, why should I not ask Herr Nordau himself to step before the looking-glass and tell us frankly whether, even in the ranks of his "psychiatrists" and lunacy doctors, he can pick out a crank more hopelessly obsessed with one idea than himself? If you want an example of echolalia, can you find a more shocking one than this gentleman who, when you say "mania," immediately begins to gabble Egomania, Graphomania, Megalomania, Onomatomania, Pyromania, Kleptomania, Dipsomania, Erotomania, Arithmomania, Oniomania, and is started off by the termination "phobia" with a string of Agoraphobia, Claustrophobia, Rupophobia, lophobia,

Nosophobia, Aichmophobia, Belenophobia, Cremnophobia, and Trichophobia? After which he suddenly observes: "This is simply philologico-medical trifling," a remark which looks like returning sanity until he follows it up by clasping his temples in the true bedlamite manner, and complaining that " psychiatry is being stuffed with useless and disturbing designations," whereas, if the psychiatrists would only listen to him, they would see that there is only one phobia and one mania: namely, degeneracy. That is, the philologico-medical triflers are not crazy enough for him. He is so utterly mad on the subject of degeneration that he finds the symptoms of it in the loftiest geniuses as plainly as in the lowest jailbirds, the exceptions being himself, Lombroso, Krafft-Ebing, Dr. Maudsley, Goethe, Shakespeare, and Beethoven. Perhaps he would have dwelt on a case so convenient in many ways for his theory as Coleridge but that it would spoil the connection between degeneration and "railway spine." If a man's senses are acute, he is degenerate, hyperæsthesia having been observed in asylums. If they are dull, he is degenerate, anaesthesia being the stigma of the craziness which made old women confess to witchcraft. If he is particular as to what he wears, he is degenerate: silk dressing-gowns and knee-breeches are grave symptoms, and woollen shirts conclusive. If he is negligent in these matters, clearly he is inattentive, and therefore degenerate. If he drinks, he is neurotic: if he is a vegetarian and teetotaller, let him be locked up at once. If he lives an evil life, that fact condemns him without further words: if on the other hand his conduct is irreproachable, he is a wretched "mattoid," incapable of the will and courage to realize his vicious propensities in action. If he writes verse, he is afflicted with echolalia; if he writes prose, he is a graphomaniac; if in his books he is tenacious of his ideas, he is obsessed; if not, he is "amorphous" and "inattentive." Wagner, as we have seen, contrived to be both obsessed and inattentive, as might be expected from one who was " himself alone charged with a greater abundance of degeneration than all the other degenerates put together." And so on and so forth.

There is, however, one sort of mental weakness, common among men who take to science, as so many people take to art, without the necessary brain power, which Nordau, with amusing unconsciousness of himself, has omitted. I mean the weakness of the man who, when his theory works out into a flagrant contradiction of the facts, concludes: "So much the worse for the facts: let them be altered," instead of: "So much the worse for my theory." What in the name of commonsense is the value of a theory which identifies Ibsen, Wagner, Tolstoy, Ruskin, and Victor Hugo with the refuse of our prisons and lunatic asylums? What is to be said of the state of mind of an inveterate pamphleteer and journalist who, instead of accepting that identification as a *reductio ad dbsurdum* of the theory, desperately sets to work to prove it by pointing out that there are numerous resemblances; that they all have heads and bodies, appetites, aberrations, whims, weaknesses, asymmetrical features, erotic impulses, fallible judgments, and the like common properties, not merely of all human beings, but all vertebrate organisms. Take Nordau's own list: "vague and incoherent thought, the tyranny of the association of ideas, the presence of obsessions, erotic excitability, religious enthusiasm, feebleness of perception, will, memory, and judgment, as well as inattention and instability." Is there a single man capable of understanding these terms who will not plead guilty to some experience of all of them, especially when he is accused vaguely and unscientifically, without any statement of the subject, or the moment, or the circumstances to which the accusation refers, or any attempt to fix a standard of sanity? I could prove Nordau to be an elephant on more evidence than he has brought to prove that our greatest men are degenerate lunatics. The papers in which Swift, having predicted the death of the sham prophet Bickerstaff on a certain date, did, after that date, immediately prove that he was dead, are much more closely and fairly reasoned than any of Nordau's chapters. And Swift, though he afterwards died in a madhouse, was too sane to be the dupe of his own logic. At that rate, where will Nordau die? Probably in a highly respectable suburban villa.

Nordau's most likeable point is the freedom and boldness with which he expresses himself. Speaking of Peladan (of whose works I know nothing), he says, whilst holding him up as a typical degenerate of the mystical variety: "His moral ideal is high and noble. He pursues with ardent hatred all that is base and vulgar, every form of egoism, falsehood, and thirst for pleasure; and his characters are thoroughly aristocratic souls, whose thoughts are concerned only with the worthiest, if somewhat exclusively artistic, interests of society." On the other hand, Maeterlinck is a "poor devil of an idiot"; Mr. W. D. O'Connor, for describing Whitman as " the good grey poet," is politely introduced as " an American driveller"; Nietzsche "belongs, body and soul, to the flock of the mangy sheep"; Ibsen is "a malignant, anti-social simpleton "; and so on. Only occasionally is he Pharisaical in his tone, as, for instance, when he becomes virtuously indignant over Wagner's dramas, and plays to Mrs. Grundy by exclaiming ironically: "How unperverted must wives and readers be, when they are in a state of mind to witness these pieces without blushing crimson and sinking into the earth for shame!" This, to do him justice, is only an exceptional lapse: a far more characteristic comment of his on Wagner's love-scenes is "The lovers in his pieces behave like tom-cats gone mad, rolling in contortions and convulsions over a root of valerian." And he is not always on the side of the police, so to speak; for he is as careless of the feelings of the " beer-drinking" German *bourgeoisie* as of those of the {esthetes. Thus, though on one page he is pointing out that Socialism and all other forms of discontent with the existing social order are " stigmata of degeneration," on the next he is talking pure Karl Marx. For example, taking the two sides in their order:

> Ibsen's egomania assumes the form of Anarchism. He is in a state of constant revolt against all that exists. ... The psychological roots of his anti-social impulses are well known. They are the degenerate's incapacity for self-adaptation, and the resultant discomfort in the midst of circumstances to which, in consequence of his organic deficiencies, he cannot accommodate himself. "The criminal," says Lombroso, "through his neurotic and impulsive nature, and his hatred of the institutions which have punished or imprisoned him, is a perpetual latent political rebel, who finds in insurrection the means, not only of satisfying his passions, but of even having them countenanced for the first time by a numerous public."

Wagner is a declared Anarchist. . . . He betrays that mental condition which the degenerate shares with enlightened reformers, born criminals with the martyrs of human progress: namely, deep, devouring discontent with existing facts. . . . He would like to crush "political and criminal civilization," as he calls it.

Now for Nordau speaking for himself:

Is it not the duty of intelligent philanthropy and justice, without destroying civilization, to adopt a better system of economy and transform the artisan from a factory convict, condemned to misery and ill-health, into a free producer of wealth, who enjoys the fruits of his labor himself, and works no more than is compatible with his health and his claims on life?

Every gift that a man receives from some other man without work, without reciprocal service, is an alms, and as such is deeply immoral.

Not in the impossible " return to Nature" lies healing for human misery, but in the reasonable organization of our struggle with nature—I might say, in universal and obligatory service against it, from which only the crippled should be exempted.

In England it was Tolstoy's sexual morality that excited the greatest interest; for in that country economic reasons condemn a formidable number of girls, particularly of the educated classes, to forego marriage;

and, from a theory which honored chastity as the highest dignity and noblest human destiny, and branded marriage with gloomy wrath as abominable depravity, these poor creatures would naturally derive rich consolation for their lonely, empty lives and their cruel exclusion from the possibility of fulfilling their natural calling.

So it appears that Nordau, too, shares "the degenerate's incapacity for self-adaptation, and the resultant discomfort in the midst of circumstances to which, in consequence of his organic deficiencies, he cannot accommodate himself." Is he not, indeed, the author of Conventional Lies of Civilization? But he has his usual easy way out of the dilemma. If Ibsen and Wagner are dissatisfied with the world, that is because the world is too good for them; but, if Max Nordau is dissatisfied, it is because Max is too good for the world. His modesty does not permit him to draw the distinction in these exact terms. Here is his statement of it:

Discontent shows itself otherwise in the degenerate than in reformers. The latter grow angry over real evils only, and make rational proposals for their remedy which are in advance of the time: these remedies may presuppose a better and wiser humanity than actually exists; but at least they are capable of being defended on reasonable grounds. The degenerate, on the other hand, selects among the arrangements of civilization such as are either immaterial or distinctly suitable, in order to rebel against them. His fury has either ridiculously insignificant aims, or simply beats the air. He either gives no earnest thought to improvement, or hatches astoundingly mad projects for 'making the world happy. His fundamental frame of mind is persistent rage against everything and everyone, which he displays in venomous phrases, savage threats, and the destructive mania of wild beasts. *Wagner is a good specimen of this species.*

Wagner was named because the passage occurs in the almost incredibly foolish chapter which is headed with his name. In another chapter it might have been Ibsen, or Tolstoy, or Ruskin, or William Morris, or any other eminent artist who shares Nordau's objection, and yours and mine, to our existing social arrangements. In the face of this, it is really impossible to deny oneself the fun of asking Nordau, with all possible good humor, who he is and what he is, that he should rail in this fashion at great men. Wagner was discontented with the condition of musical art in Europe. In essay after essay he pointed out with the most laborious exactitude what it was he complained of, and how it might be remedied. He not only shewed, in the teeth of the most envenomed opposition from all the dunderheads, pedants, and vested interests in Europe, what the musical drama ought to be as a work of art, but how theatres for its proper performance should be managed—nay, how they should be built, down to the arrangement of the seats and the position of the instruments in the orchestra. And he not only shewed this on paper, but he successfully composed the music dramas, built a model theatre, gave the model performances, *did* the impossible;

so that there is now nobody left, not even Hanslick, who cares to stultify himself by repeating the old anti-Wagner cry of craziness and Impossibilism—nobody, save only Max Nordau, who, like a true journalist, is fact-proof. William Morris objected to the abominable ugliness of early Victorian decoration and furniture, to the rhymed rhetoric which did duty for poetry from the Renaissance to the nineteenth century, to kamptulicon stained glass, and, later on, to the shiny commercial gentility of typography according to the American ideal, which was being spread through England by Harper's Magazine and The Century, and which had not, like your abolition of "justification" in Liberty, the advantage of saving trouble. Well, did he sit down, as Nordau suggests, to rail helplessly at the men who were at all events getting the work of the world done, however inartistically? Not a bit of it: he designed and manufactured the decorations he wanted, and furnished and decorated houses with them; he put into public halls and churches tapestries and picture-windows which cultivated people now travel to see as they travel to see first-rate fifteenth-century work in that kind; the books from his Kelmscott Press, printed with type designed by his own hand, are pounced on by collectors like the treasures of our national museums, all this work, remember, involving the successful conducting of a large business establishment and factory, and being relieved by the incidental production of a series of poems and prose romances which placed their author in the position of the greatest living English poet. Now let me repeat the terms in which Nordau describes this kind of activity. "Ridiculously insignificant aims—beating the air—no earnest thought to improvement—astoundingly mad projects for making the world happy—persistent rage against everything and everyone, displayed in venomous phrases, savage threats, and destructive mania of wild beasts." Is there not something deliciously ironical in the ease with which a splenetic pamphleteer, with nothing to shew for himself except a bookful of blunders tacked on to a mock scientific theory picked up at second hand from a few lunacy doctors with a literary turn, should be able to create a European scandal by declaring that the greatest creative artists of the century are barren and hysterical madmen? I do not know what the American critics have said about Nordau; but here the tone has been that there is much in what he says, and that he is evidently an authority on the subjects with which he deals. And yet I assure you, on my credit as a man who lives by art criticism, that from his preliminary description of a Morris design as one "on which strange birds flit among crazily ramping branches, and blowzy flowers coquet with vain butterflies" (which is about as sensible as a description of the Norman chapel in the Tower of London as a characteristic specimen of Baroque architecture would be) to his coupling of Cimabue and Fra Angelico as primitive Florentine masters; from his unashamed bounce about "the conscientious observance of the laws of counterpoint" by Beethoven and other masters celebrated for breaking them, to his unlucky shot about "a pedal bass with correct harmonization" (a pedal bass happening to be the particular instance in which even the professor-made rules of "correct harmonization" are suspended), Nordau exposes his sciolism time after time us an authority upon the fine arts. But his critics, being for the most part ignorant literary men like himself, with sharpened wits and neglected eyes and ears, have swallowed Cimabue and Ghirlandajo and the pedal bass like so many gulls. Here an Ibsen admirer may maintain that Ibsen is an exception to the degenerate theory and should be classed with Goethe; there a Wagnerite may plead that Wagner is entitled to the honors of Beethoven; elsewhere one may find a champion of Rossetti venturing cautiously to suggest a suspicion of the glaringly obvious fact that Nordau has read only the two or three popular ballads like The Blessed Damozel, Eden Bower, Sister Helen, and so on, which every smatterer reads, and that his knowledge of the mass of pictorial, dramatic, and decorative work turned out. by Rossetti, Burne-Jones, Ford Madox Brown, William Morris, and Holman Hunt, without a large knowledge and careful study of which no man can possibly speak with any critical authority of the pre-Raphaelite movement, is apparently limited to a glance at Holman Hunt's Shadow of the Cross, or possibly an engraving thereof. But in the main he is received as a serious authority on his subjects; and that is why we too, without malice and solely as a matter of public duty, are compelled to take all this trouble to destroy him.

And now, my dear Tucker, I have told you as much about Nordau's book as it is worth. In a country where art was really known to the people, instead of being merely read about, it would not be necessary to spend three lines on such a work. But in England, where nothing but superstitious awe and self-mistrust prevents most men from thinking about art as Nordau boldly speaks about it; where to have a sense of art is to be one in a thousand, the other nine hundred and ninety-nine being either Philistine voluptuaries or Calvinistic anti-voluptuaries, it is useless to pretend that Nordau's errors will be self-evident. Already we have native writers, without half his cleverness or energy of expression, clumsily imitating his sham scientific vivisection in their attacks on artists whose work they happen to dislike. Therefore, in riveting his book to the counter, I have used a nail long enough to go through a few pages by other people as well; and that must be my excuse for my disregard of the familiar editorial stigma of degeneracy which Nordau calls Agoraphobia, or Fear of Space.

www.ingramcontent.com/pod-product-compliance
Lightning Source LLC
Chambersburg PA
CBHW021015180526
45163CB00005B/1963